MS-#110 $10.00

Decorating
Vintage Style

COUNTRY LIVING

Decorating
Vintage Style

Using Romantic Fabrics and Flea Market Finds

CHRISTINA STRUTT

HEARST BOOKS
A DIVISION OF STERLING PUBLISHING CO., INC.
NEW YORK

Library of Congress Cataloging-in-Publication Data
Strutt, Christina.
    Decorating vintage style: using romantic fabrics and fleamarket finds
/Christina Strutt.
        p. cm.
Includes index
    ISBN 1-58816-240-0
  1. House furnishings. 2. Interior decoration. 3. Textile fabrics in interior decoration. I. Title.
    TX311 .S834 2003
    747--dc21

                                                                2002153856

10 9 8 7 6 5 4 3 2 1

Published by Hearst Books
A Division of Sterling Publishing Co., Inc.
387 Park Avenue South, New York, N.Y. 10016

First published in 2003 by Cico Books Ltd.

Country Living and Hearst Books are trademarks owned by
Hearst Magazines Property, Inc., in USA, and Hearst Communications, Inc., in Canada.

www.countryliving.com

Distributed in Canada by Sterling Publishing
c/o Canadian Manda Group, One Atlantic Avenue, Suite 105
Toronto, Ontario, Canada M6K 3E7
Distributed in Australia by Capricorn Link (Australia) Pty. Ltd.
P.O. Box 704, Windsor, NSW 2756 Australia

Printed in the USA

ISBN 1-58816-240-0

Edited by Sarah Hoggett
Photography by Edina van der Wyck
Designed by Christine Wood

contents

foreword

Home is the one place that I look to for beauty and comfort for myself and my family. And, since the comforts of home, at least for me, are associated with things from the past, I do have a special fondness for all things vintage. Pretty floral fabrics, beautifully aged furniture, inherited collections, and colors reminiscent of years past, all help to bring a sense of nostalgia and personality to any home—new or old.

In this book we take a look at the beauty and appeal that Decorating Vintage Style has to offer and how appropriate it is for the way we live our lives today. As you'll see in the pages that follow, vintage style pays homage to the past with its eclectic mix of furnishings and fabrics, yet provides a fresh new twist on tradition. It values style and beauty over expense. And, it provides an easy way of bringing a relaxed elegance and casual comfort to any room of the house.

Whether you have furnishings and collections passed down from a parent or relative or continue to shop at flea markets and yard sales in search of that lucky find, this book will not only inspire you, but also provide you with a renewed appreciation for all things vintage.

NANCY MERNIT SORIANO
EDITOR-IN-CHIEF, *COUNTRY LIVING*

the romance of vintage

Vintage is an instantly recognizable style of decorating that manages to be both timeless and contemporary, comfortingly familiar to all of us and yet uniquely personal to whoever put those particular pieces together. Always eclectic, often a little eccentric, it is a soft, romantic style that embodies our nostalgia for days gone by. Faded fabrics printed with roses; everyday household items from white enamel pitchers to colored glass bottles; battered toys that bear the marks of generations of children's love: this chapter looks at why vintage has such an enduring appeal.

Above left: A linen sheet, drying in the sun, is laid on lavender bushes so that it soaks up the scent of the flowers.

Above right: Floral-printed towels and a lovely enamel pitcher and bowl make an early-morning wash a delight.

Right: In the bedroom area of our tent, the calico lining and muslin bed canopy billow in the breeze.

In my view, rooms without decoration are like a dinner without food or a canvas without paint. Thankfully, after a recent short-lived excursion into minimalism, both interior designers and the public at large seem to be turning back to coziness, color, and clutter—and no style is better suited to this, or more versatile, than vintage.

The resurgence of minimalism was, I think, a reaction against the decorative excesses of the 1980s, when we were encouraged to stencil everything in sight and to drape our windows with great swags and swathes. Minimalism rescued us from our own indulgences: we emptied our closets and drawers of fripperies and keepsakes, replaced the warmth of antique oak and pine with cool granite and hard-edged steel, and turned to bare white walls in place of rag-rolled and sponged colorwashes. With no room for sentimentality, mementos of the past had no place in the cleansed and feng shuied spaces to which we were all meant to aspire.

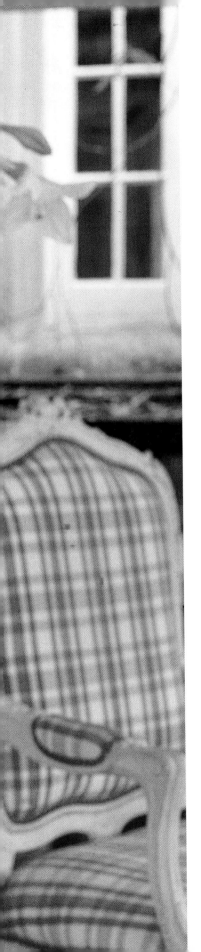

Left: Cut flowers, displayed in an assortment of containers, wait to be placed around the house.

Above left: Small and large flowers mingle together in a delightfully natural-looking display, and even sculpturally shaped vegetables such as artichokes can be as beautiful as any bloom.

Above right: An antique linen sheet, printed with our "Hatley Rose" design, makes a ravishing tablecloth, blending with the cut flowers rather than detracting from them.

In aspiring to minimalism, we were throwing the baby out with the bath water. Pristine, sparkling surfaces that have been cleared not only of clutter but also of any sign of the owner's personality and interests may look all very well in the pages of a glossy style magazine, but how many of us would truly feel comfortable living in such a setting? After a hard day's work, all most of us want to do is kick off our shoes, curl up in a comfortable armchair or sofa, and relax—not feel as if we ought to put on a new designer outfit in order to live up to the same standard as the furnishings! And where do children and the trappings of family life fit into such a scenario? Sticky fingermarks, felt-tip scribbles, and rainbow-colored jumbles of toys are positively taboo, while a lively toddler in the same room as a low-level table bearing an exquisite but fragile *objet d'art* is a disaster waiting to happen.

*Left: A hotchpotch of
china, glass, and
silver candlesticks
muddle formal
with rustic.*

Right: Sometimes at night, candles burning outside in the wind are a little unruly. Small old-fashioned oil lamps give a lovely soothing glow.

Below right: A table in the tent set for summer tea. Baking coordinating cakes may be taking things a little too far, but it makes for a pretty picture!

Now, the pendulum has swung back full tilt—though, in truth, vintage style never really went away completely. Vintage has atmosphere in abundance. It has a kind of faded charm, a used and lived-in look that is the complete antithesis of cold and clinical minimalism. Fabrics are soft and natural—linens, cottons, and muslins rather than synthetic polyesters and rayons. The designs, too, are often drawn from the natural world, with old-fashioned roses and other cottage-garden flowers being a common theme. Objects are often functional as well as decorative, but they have an inherent beauty that we respond to instinctively.

When we look at vintage, we're aware of the generations that have gone before, of lives loved and lost, of possessions treasured. We feel at ease in vintage-style interiors, partly because of their coziness and comfort, and partly because the objects evoke a nostalgia for what we perceive as more carefree, innocent days.

This is the feeling I've tried to create, both in my own home and in my company, Cabbages & Roses. I hope that the photographs in this book, many of which were taken in my home (or, in this chapter, in the marquee that functions as an extension to our house during the summer months) will demonstrate what I mean by vintage style and encourage you to try out similar ideas in your own home.

Right: A Louis-XIV-style armchair sits rather grandly next to a small side table carrying a basket with a motley collection of household items. On the beautifully carved bench on the right, old vintage quilts and cushions covered with scraps of vintage fabric mingle with a bright, modern gingham to create a happy and lively design that is far more relaxed and informal than one based around a single fabric design could ever be.

vintage fabrics

Fabric is one of the most distinctive and instantaneous ways of transforming any decorating scheme, and vintage fabrics have a timeless quality that allows them to look good in almost any setting. Unless they have been hidden away from the light and never used, original vintage fabrics tend to look slightly faded, and this is undoubtedly part of their charm. Fabrics that would once have been brightly colored, such as floral chintzes with a vibrant red background, may now be dulled to a rich and slightly threadbare pink —perhaps the textile equivalent of the kind of patina that one sees and reveres on antique wood.

Hand-woven fabrics are becoming increasingly rare and expensive, but you may well be lucky enough to find pieces in junk stores or at fleamarkets. The antique linen that we use at Cabbages & Roses was mostly made in France, woven into narrow widths that needed to be stitched together to be turned into sheets. It is the hand-made and slightly battered appearance that appeals: when we are offered sheets that have been patched, we find it difficult to conceal our excitement. Even the tiniest of scraps can be stitched together and made into all kinds of useful and decorative items, from needle cases to cushion covers.

Linen and chintz are not the only fabrics available: cotton and muslin are lightweight alternatives. Vintage ticking from old mattress covers allows you to use stylish stripes in a variety of colors, while country-style ginghams and warm plaids provide timeless checks that contrast wonderfully well with some of the more elaborate floral designs.

Left: Our tent allows us to combine the coziness of being surrounded by familiar objects and creature comforts with the liberating experience of outdoor living. Here, the fat and comfortable ticking-covered cushions on a sofa or daybed are reflected in a simple mirror bought many years ago from a fleamarket.

Never be afraid to combine different fabrics in a decorating scheme: mixing and matching fabrics invariably looks more stylish than using a single fabric for everything. Coordination can be taken too far.

Recycling fabrics, either by making simple repairs or by cutting things up and making something else from them, is one of the pleasures of vintage style: what could be simpler or more effective than giving a tatty old cushion or chair seat a new lease of life with a new cover? Trimmings, too, can be removed and used to adorn tablecloths and pillowslips, and a glass jar full of antique buttons makes an attractive display in its own right.

Of course, not everyone is lucky enough to be able to find (or afford) genuine vintage fabrics. Modern fabrics printed with antique-style designs often turn out to be perfectly suited to vintage interiors—so, if you can't find an original fabric to suit your needs, it's worth remembering that a wide range of reproduction fabrics is now available.

Left: A rose-printed muslin mosquito net, draped from a branch of a tree, provides a dappled oasis of calm in a corner of the garden. Furnished with no more than a small linen-covered mattress and an organza pillow, this is a truly romantic summer haven that can be recreated almost anywhere there is a tree, a piece of grass, and that all-important touch of summer sunshine.

sheer romance

As well as being cozy and comforting, vintage fabrics can also provide a form of escapism, by creating an environment that is far removed from everyday life. Muslin must surely be one of the simplest and most effective fabrics in this respect. Sheer enough for light to penetrate yet opaque enough to shield you from prying eyes at the same time, it diffuses the light so that everything appears to be bathed in a translucent haze. So soft and light that it can be stirred by the slightest breeze, it has a unique dreamlike quality, implying a sensuous world far removed from the trials and tribulations of our daily existence.

Because of the way in which light streams through it, muslin is the perfect fabric for lightweight summer drapes in almost any room of the house, from chic sitting room to children's nursery. But why stop at using it for window treatments? A muslin canopy will turn any bedroom into a romantic boudoir, and I can think of no more beautiful a way to while away a summer afternoon than to rest beneath a tree within the soft folds of a mosquito net, such as the one shown on these pages. Whether it's plain white or patterned with a vintage-style floral pattern, such as the one shown here, muslin is the ultimate in femininity and sophisticated romance. If it's a secret haven you're looking for, then muslin is the means with which to create it.

Left: A tiny covered porch houses a multitude of garden tools, flowers, pots, and baskets, with roses resplendent in an old tin bucket.

Right: A side table used as a storage area, displays rather than merely accommodates items that are in daily use.

vintage treasures

One of the things we associate most strongly with vintage style are eclectic displays of objects from days gone by, when mass production meant making hundreds, rather than millions, of items that possess an individuality that is sadly lacking from many of today's products. Colored glassware, pretty china plates and dishes, children's toys in their original packaging, kitchen utensils and storage jars: anything can be grist to the vintage stylist's mill. The best of these displays manage to turn the ordinary into the extraordinary and open our eyes to the inherent beauty of the objects—a beauty that has nothing whatsoever to do with the monetary value of the items, but depends entirely on the skill with which they are combined.

Bric-a-brac used with thought and inventiveness can change a house into a home, blending bland landscapes into a gallery of amusements and distractions. My own personal criterion of whether a room is successful or not is to imagine myself lying there with a dose of flu—not seriously ill, but not well enough to occupy my time reading, or painting, or sewing. Is there enough to hold my interest and distract me from my fever?

I use the word "amusements" very deliberately, for I think it's always a mistake for interior design to take itself too seriously. A little quirkiness and eccentricity, unexpected juxtapositions of objects that bring a smile to the viewer's face, should always be encouraged!

The objects you have around you may bring happy memories flooding back, either because they are objects that you have inherited from loved ones or because they remind you of your childhood. They may simply be objects that you've fallen in love with and bought for no other reason than that. However, I firmly believe that you should always surround yourself with things that speak to you on a personal level.

Left: A small folding stool serves as a handy side table for afternoon tea when lazing in these stylish deckchairs.

Below left: A plant is only a weed if it happens to be growing where you don't want it to grow. Here, bindweed adorns a battered and peeling old iron bench.

Below right: White sneakers—the only footwear one needs in summer, in my opinion—dry in the sun.

Vintage style is not about the monetary value of objects. People often ask me how much something is "worth"—and my view is that if you love it, it's worth whatever you're prepared to pay for it. And if you're talking about things that you've inherited from family and friends, then who can put a price on sentimental value? Even chipped and slightly damaged items have their place in a vintage-style interior: a few scratches and cracks are a small price to pay for something that evokes the past with such resonance.

When it comes to displaying your vintage treasures, a good rule of thumb is to start with the object that you love most and then add other items around it. You might have a specific theme that suits the function of the room—say, cooking utensils in a kitchen, or models of boats and seashells in a bathroom. It may be something that relates to your pastimes, such as reels and bobbins and other sewing paraphernalia, or old theater posters. Or you might chose to arrange your display by color, putting together a miscellaneous collection of items in related shades of blues and greens, or reds and yellows. But whatever the rationale, every successful display needs some kind of unifying factor.

If you have so many items that you can't possibly display them all at once, ring the changes every few months: take some things out of storage, and put others away for a while. You'll have the thrill of rediscovering old friends and revamping your home at the same time—and it's a lot cheaper and quicker than redecorating!

Left: A vintage garden chair, with wheels at the back for easy repositioning, has its contours softened by the addition of a home-made gingham cushion.

Right: Summer skirts blowing in the breeze: hanging laundry to dry in the garden scents our clothes with the perfume of newly-mown grass.

Left: What could be simpler—or more enchanting—than this tent made by simply throwing a piece of sturdy canvas over a length of washing line? Whether it's a play tent in which the children can act out tales of adventure and derring-do or the setting for a sophisticated picnic of strawberries, cream, and (why not?) a bottle of vintage champagne, it harks back to bygone days when the world was a more carefree and innocent place, and summers seemed to last for ever.

Left and right: Comfortable cushions, a good book, and a plentiful supply of cooling drinks are all you need to turn the tent into a peaceful haven in which to while away a few precious hours between domestic chores. A pocket at each corner, lined with a heavy weight, anchors the tent to the ground.

In gathering material for this book, I realized that the houses in which I have always felt comfortable and welcome are not necessarily those in which a great deal of money has been spent. Quite the contrary: it is time, thought, and inventiveness that have created the atmosphere. Each house that we photographed is unique—something that would have been difficult to achieve if the homes had been furnished with mass-produced items available in every high street or shopping center.

This, perhaps, is the whole point of a vintage lifestyle. It is achieved purely by instinct, unhindered by fashion, gauged by visual and heartfelt pleasure. I hope that this book will encourage you to hunt out treasures of your own. The photographs may spark off ideas on how to display your own collections and treasures; they may even inspire you to haunt salerooms, comb through dusty junk stores, and rise at the crack of dawn to find those fleamarket treasures before anyone else does. But remember: the best—the *only*—reason for allowing something into your home is that you love it for its beauty, despite any imperfections it may have.

vintage kitchens

A great deal of time and money is spent on fitted kitchens nowadays—understandably, since most modern kitchens are very small and we need to make maximum use of the space available. But, as you will see in the following pages, lack of space is no reason to join the hordes of people with identical kitchens. Vintage free-standing furniture and cooking utensils that have stood the test of time have so much more charm than acres of melamine and plastic. An old-fashioned kitchen is the hub of family life: pots of home-made jam proudly displayed on a shelf will more than make up for a soufflé that refuses to rise, while ranks of shining copper, gleaming glassware, and pretty serving dishes will inspire even the most reluctant cook to don an apron and set to work with gusto.

decorative details

Most kitchen utensils are attractive enough to be decorative as well as functional, so instead of hiding them away in cupboards, why not make a feature of them and allow them to be seen in all their glory? Even the most mundane objects can look stunning if a little thought is given to the way they are displayed. Think of the magnificent still-life paintings of Old Masters such as Rembrandt and then look around your own kitchen: rough wicker baskets; simple vintage bowls with the most elegant lines and curves; humble wooden spoons massed together in a stoneware jar or plain white pitcher; the potential for beautiful still-life compositions is everywhere, even if you never pick up a paintbrush. Establish a core, year-round display of, say, china and copper pans, and add other elements with the changing seasons—perhaps wicker baskets of vegetables in summer, or nuts and berries in the fall.

Opposite left: Incongruous details— the miniature bucket and set of child's garden shears in the photo (far left) and the giant conch shell (left)—add humor and individuality to a display.

Right: In this eclectic collection of kitchen utensils, each piece is beautiful in its own right, decorative as well as practical.

Old storage tins in which tea, coffee, and other foodstuffs were sold, make wonderful decorative items: manufacturers put a lot of effort and money into designing attractive packaging and these tins are, if anything, even more attractive than the disposable packaging we have to endure now.

The important thing is to make sure that each object has enough space around it to allow it to stand out from its surroundings, and having a plain, or neutral-colored, background is one way of achieving this. Contrasts of texture—perhaps smooth glassware on a roughly hewn shelf, or shiny metal utensils hanging on a matte, painted wall—are essential. Think also about the scale of different elements and aim for a balance.

Although exuberant jumbles of objects are a feature of vintage style, a cluttered kitchen is not necessarily an untidy one: in a well-organized kitchen, every item should have its place and its purpose. Although I may appear somewhat frivolous, I make sure that every object that I bring home from fleamarkets (well, *almost* every object!) has a use.

Left: Every item on this pine side table has at least one purpose—even the aerial on the vintage-style radio, which not only brings the radio waves into the kitchen but also supports the orchid which has grown too tall to bear its own weight.

Below left: A galvanized tin bucket holds waste for the compost heap.
Below right: A lovely beaded jug cover, hand made from scraps of vintage fabric, is preferable to plastic food wrap.

Above: A rich and varied collection of kitchen treasures, collected over many years, is assembled in a style that is unique to its owner.

Right: Kitchen china is in constant use. Housing it on open shelving makes it easy to find and easy to put away and is very a practical way to avoid standard fitted kitchen cabinets.

simple storage

Kitchen manufacturers would have us believe that fitted cabinets are the answer to all our storage problems, but how sterile and soulless they are! How much more pleasing it is to gaze on colorful, serried ranks of bottles and jars of home-made preserves and neat rows of china plates. And how much easier it is to find what you need when everything is in full view.

Kitchen dressers are perhaps the ideal solution, as you can keep rarely used items tucked away in the lower half and everyday crockery and utensils on the shelves. But even inexpensive ready-made shelves can easily be customized to suit your tastes and style.

Left: Lack of space and lots of china need not necessarily add up to an untidy and inefficient kitchen—in fact, having bowls and pots within easy reach on open shelves makes the cook's life much simpler.

Above left: Dressers are wonderfully versatile, attractive in their own right yet invaluable for storage and display purposes.

Above right: An old wooden plate rack is a great way of storing lots of crockery in a small space, while attaching hooks to the underside of shelves is another useful way of maximizing storage space for cups and pitchers.

Right: An impressive display of well-used cooking utensils that are visually pleasing as well as practical: who wouldn't feel inspired to cook in a kitchen like this!

Small hooks can be attached to the edge or underside of shelves to hold cups and mugs, and magnetic strips screwed to walls or deep shelf edges to hold knives and other metal utensils. Another simple solution is to place butcher's hooks (S-shaped hooks available in a range of sizes) on a simple metal or wooden bar, or even on a home-made wooden frame over which you've stretched chicken wire, and hang up anything from strings of onions or garlic to egg whisks, corkscrews, and even recipes cut from magazines. To prevent the shelves from looking overly utilitarian, soften them by adding a simple fabric shelf edging, such as the one shown in the photograph on page 53: this is a lovely way to add color and interest to a plain surface.

country colors

Color is, of course, a very personal choice, but I feel that certain colors work better in country-style kitchens than others. With the emphasis on home-cooked and home-grown produce, naturally occurring colors such as greens and browns seem to work particularly well. White or off-white walls, or perhaps creams and yellows, are useful light background colors for displaying collections: somehow, strong, modern colors would seem out of place in a country kitchen. I have always shied away from using large amounts of blue in kitchens, but that's because blue can look very cold in the harsh, gray light of the chilly region where I live. However in a climate where the natural light lends a warmer tone, a rich azure blue would have a very different feel: choose your colors with very careful regard for the quality and direction of daylight.

Opposite left: An old jam jar with a green gingham lid will perform many decorative storage functions in its long life.

Opposite right: A collection of old French coffee cups, decorated with green stripes and checks.

Below: A wooden bowl full of meringues shares space with a jam jar filled with old-fashioned roses.

Right: An old meat safe is now used as a china store, the contents clearly visible behind the wire in the doors.

Left and above: I'm a firm believer in using fresh flowers wherever possible: they bring not only color but also life to a room. In the photographs on these two pages, large-bloomed hydrangeas and roses in subtle shades of lilac and cream are massed in simple containers to great effect: they immediately draw the eye, while their fragrance pervades the room and lifts the spirits.

Large expanses of walls painted in a light or neutral color need to be broken up with accents of a contrasting color. Lilac and pink are often good choices for a kitchen: they are warm without being overpowering, subtle but strong enough to make an impact, and they bring to mind the cheering colors of summer and sweet-scented roses and lavender. A strategically placed vase of flowers, a cushion, or a hand-painted china bowl will "lift" the room and prevent it from looking bland and uninteresting.

If you need something to contrast more strongly with greens and browns, red is a good choice. Red is the complementary of green, and artists have exploited the use of complementary colors for centuries. Don't overdo it, though: a little goes a long way. A splash of color contrast—perhaps a red dishtowel draped over a chair back—is sufficient.

egg

Above: An old, glazed bowl is filled with lovely brown eggs.

Right: Artist Lucy Fry's kitchen, with sumptuous cooking ingredients from all over the world, supplies a visual as well as a culinary feast.

food for thought

A real working kitchen should combine cooking utensils and foodstuffs in its decoration—gleaming saucepans, wooden spoons, eggs, herbs, oils, wines all in full view within easy and inspiring access. There is always something a little suspicious about a clean and sparse kitchen, with acres of granite and steel and not a jar or spice or spoon to be seen. How on earth can you prepare a meal when all the ingredients and tools have been hidden away to avoid disrupting a slick, minimalist interior? To me, the simple beauty of a bowl of eggs, or elegant bottles of the finest olive oil steeped with herbs, or mounds of brightly colored citrus fruits, is testament to the fact that the owner of that kitchen appreciates fine food—and I know that any meals prepared there will be cooked with love and enthusiasm.

Left: A lovely corner of Lucy Fry's kitchen has an unexpected ensemble of vintage pieces. Simplicity is the key: the gingham tablecloth and red geranium add a hint of color to offset the white walls, while an old painting of the Madonna gazing down on the room and its occupants evokes a feeling of peace and serenity.

kitchen dining

Furnished organically with functional pots, pans, and foodstuffs as well as more unexpected items like grand paintings and prints, the eclectic style of a country-house kitchen makes it the most welcoming room in the house. I love the informality of eating in the kitchen rather than in a separate dining room: warm and cozy, with delicious smells filling the room, the atmosphere is wonderfully relaxed and inviting. It's also a lovely way of making guests feel part of your family: when everyone's in the kitchen, caught up in the hustle and bustle of food preparation, no one needs to be stuffy, and formal, or on their "best behavior."

The one drawback, of course, is that cooking inevitably creates chaos and clutter—and if you're not a very confident cook, you have to be prepared to put up with people peering over your shoulder offering "helpful" advice. It's such a shame that very few houses nowadays have the luxury of an old-fashioned scullery, where dirty pots and pans can be stowed out of sight—but what price a little untidiness compared with the pleasure of breaking bread with family and friends?

Country kitchens tend to work best when very simply decorated, with plain white or neutral-colored walls. Stone flags or wooden boards (either left in their natural state or painted with a light colorwash) are the most obvious choices of flooring. Well-placed rugs make a warm and welcoming sight, though choose ones that can be easily cleaned as spillages are inevitable, no matter how careful you are. Vintage-style cotton and rag rugs are readily available; you may even be lucky enough to come across them in a junk store or fleamarket.

If space allows, it's lovely to dedicate an area of the kitchen to the children. Scaled-down children's furniture is perfect for youngsters who want to invite their friends to a tea party, while budding chefs will love being able to carry out simple tasks like cutting cookies or spreading icing on cakes.

Above: The scullery of a country kitchen is curtained off with a piece of vintage fabric.

Left: This kitchen has an old-fashioned look, but is still practical enough for a modern home.

Using fabric is a wonderful way of transforming a workmanlike kitchen table into an informal dining area. For a kitchen dining table that is used for cooking as well as for eating, oilcloth is a good choice. As well as being a practical choice in a kitchen, printed oilcloth can be every bit as beautiful as a traditional cotton cloth; its wipe-clean surface makes life so much simpler as a tablecloth often lasts for no more than one sitting before a spillage of red wine or tomato ketchup ruins its pristine state.

Fabric can be used to soften other utilitarian areas in the kitchen, too. Instead of smooth cupboard doors, why not hang a simple gingham curtain over the opening to hide away little-used kitchen equipment or even the garbage can.

Right: This dining room is light and cozy, and filled with pretty and delicate furniture and decoration. Although it is created for formal dining, it is anything but oppressive and serious.

Rooms that are set aside for dining only and furnished with heavy, formal furniture seem to me to be rather sad and neglected places. They are usually used only for grand occasions and I am filled with dread at the thought of having to spend an entire evening imprisoned at table, making polite conversation and counting the minutes until I can make my escape.

If you treat it carefully, however, a dining room need not be oppressive and grand: avoid the traditional, dark furniture and austere, serious paintings. Opt instead for pale-colored and pretty tablecloths, upholstery, and window treatments; bring in mirrors and elegant candlesticks to enhance the sense of light in the room; arrange cut flowers in white china or unfussy glass containers; and the whole mood changes from being gloomy and rather forbidding to airy and carefree.

When a dining room has a dual purpose—if it's also used as, say, a study or a library—it immediately has a less formal atmosphere. Instead of being a room that one enters only occasionally, it becomes one that people use on a daily basis. It feels lived-in and loved, and has much more of the occupants' personal stamp on it.

vintage living

The key to decorating your living room in vintage style is, first and foremost, to decorate it for you and your family. Many rooms fail because they are furnished like a showcase, with more regard given to the impression they will make on visitors than to the people who spend time in them every day. As a result, they are rarely a true representation of the owner's personality: instead, they make a statement about what he or she thinks is expected of them. So forget about convention: furnish your room comfortably, in a way that suits you and your lifestyle, and decorate it with things of beauty that have a personal significance for you. Guests, too, will take pleasure in the warm and relaxed atmosphere that you create.

Above: A ceramic jardinière sits with a collection of nineteenth-century cow creamers in the home of painter Anthea Craigmyle.

Left: A mad jumble of treasures creates an enchanted grotto of a window seat, in which printed velvet curtains look perfectly at ease framing a stage set of lemons, a felt carrot, cracked china, and fake flowers.

eclectic elegance

Eclecticism is perhaps the most enduring—and endearing—aspect of vintage style. Anything goes! There are no rules, no rhyme or reason behind the choice of decoration, other than an instinctive affiliation with each piece on the part of the owner. I love the way these rooms evolve as the years go by: small alterations—adding or taking away a painting or a chair, a cushion or a cracked plate—may be so subtle as to pass almost unnoticed or they may be the catalyst that inspires you to reposition all the furniture and set to work with a paintbrush. The point is that precise, conscious planning is an anathema to vintage style: the rooms develop organically, almost (it seems) of their own accord.

Right: In this corner of Prudence Macleod's study, family photographs and amusing children's toys sit happily alongside pretty notebooks and businesslike files. No less than five different fabrics can be seen in this photograph: I doubt whether Prudence gave even one moment's thought as to whether they would "go" together, but the result is as near perfect as is possible.

Remember, however, that one can have too much of a good thing and that it is as important to edit your possessions as it is to add to them. Layer upon layer of too many lovely things can confuse the eye—so practice restraint with your treasures. Often, just one small object can destroy the visual balance of a group; when this happens, try to set aside any sentimental considerations and remove the offending article.

A little eccentricity often goes hand in hand with eclecticism—and why shouldn't it? If you can't indulge in a little quirkiness in the privacy of your own home, then the world has become a very sad place! Items that might be considered lacking in taste in a more serious and self-conscious style of decorating (plastic flowers, kitsch ornaments, cartoon characters, for example) can blend together wonderfully in vintage style because the overall effect is always greater than the sum of its individual parts. If an object means something to you, or even if it simply brings a smile to your face at the start of yet another dreary winter's day, then no one has the right to tell you that it's out of place.

Above: A jam jar is filled with old-fashioned roses.

Right: Even floral fabric can bring a room alive: here, cushion covers and throws are made from antique linen. They blend perfectly with a patchwork cushion cover in a pattern known as Grandmother's Flower Garden (far left) and a vintage quilt and little toile de jouy pillow (far right).

living with flowers

Flowers always breathe life into a room and I don't believe you can ever have too many. I like to mass lots of cottage-garden blooms together in a loose, informal arrangement. If you're going to mix different types, then spread them evenly throughout the arrangement rather than having a clump of one type and then another. This gives a much more natural look, like wild flowers growing in a summer meadow. Also go for odd numbers of flower types (one, three, or five different types in a vase, rather than two or four) as this creates a better visual balance, and mix tiny flowers such as baby's breath with larger ones like tea roses or hydrangeas. Think about the scale of the arrangement, too: a huge container can look very dramatic if there aren't too many other things near by, but a jam jar or chipped mug filled with wild flowers on a window ledge or small side table looks equally effective and is on a much more intimate scale.

Left: It's hard to believe, but Katie Forman has furnished this farmhouse sitting room almost entirely from junk-store finds, and bits and pieces that she has inherited over the years. The result is a peaceful haven, stylish but not austere. Flowers, real and artificial, adorn almost every surface, from the tiny rose on the chimney breast and the informal swag along the mantel to the floral-patterned upholstery fabrics, screen, and rug.

Above: Mr. Moon, the purr-fect cat sits on a George III-style gilt armchair in the home of painter Anthea Craigmyle.

Left: Comfort and beauty combined: squashy cotton-covered cushions invite you to sink into the sofa, while the elegant window treatments are models of restraint and good taste.

comfort zone

John Fowler, one half of the famed decorating duo Colefax and Fowler, once said that decoration is a logical compromise between comfort and beauty. Personally, I see no reason why you should ever need to compromise: the two go hand in hand and can be made to blend seamlessly. But it does reinforce the point that decorating is about creating rooms that are to be lived in, not viewed as museum galleries to be walked through on tiptoe while talking in hushed voices.

Left and right:
Perched on a table in
the home of artist
Lucy Fry, this
handsome, generously
framed old mirror
reflects the white-
painted walls of the
room. Below, a
charming and
apparently casually
arranged still life of
teapots, an old tin
that once contained
Turkish delight, and a
vintage bowl full of
hand-painted eggs
bring a warm and
personal touch to a
room that might
otherwise seem
rather austere.

reflected glory

Mirrors are a wonderful way of bringing drama and light into a room and making it seem much bigger than it really is. In my view, the larger the mirror, the better. I still hanker after the pale, carved, wood-framed mirror that filled an entire wall at my ballet class too many years ago to mention, but sadly the doors and windows of our tiny cottage are so small that we'd never be able to squeeze such a monster inside.

Old mirrors can be bought at auction for very little; even if the frames have seen better days, it's really very easy to paint or gild them to give them a new lease of life, and a few silver spots on the glass add character and are nothing to worry about.

Right: An ornate, cast-iron, Victorian fireplace is painted white. The tongue-and-groove paneling on the wall above adds warmth to the room, both physically and aesthetically.

Left: A fine muslin curtain allows the sunlight to penetrate while providing a degree of privacy.

Of course, there are other ways of making a room seem more light and airy. What better way to make use of a room's natural light than to drape fine muslin curtains from a simple painted pole? The fabric is so fine that bright sunlight simply pours through it; at the same time, it diffuses and spreads the light so that, even on dull days, the room will appear to be bathed in a soft haze.

Brilliant white walls can look too harsh and clinical, but there are many shades of off-white paint available which reflect light and give a sense of airiness just as well without being as cold. However, large expanses of smooth, unadorned plaster would bring any room perilously close to my personal *bête noire* of minimalism, so try to give your walls some kind of textural contrast—tongue-and-groove paneling is a good choice.

When it comes to showing off ornaments in settings like this, it's definitely a case of "less is more"—even the simplest of ornaments can have dramatic impact when displayed singly.

period charm

When people move home, one of their most common mistakes is to make sweeping changes to the décor. You need to live in a house for a while before you can get a feel for its character. Find out if you've inherited any period features. Find out what colors would have been in vogue when the house was originally built: even if you would never previously have considered using them, you might find that they're perfect for the house. See how light affects the mood of rooms at different times of the day. Only when you've established this basic decorating framework should you think about details such as ornaments.

Left: Painted a lovely shade of celadon, the cupboard, shutters, and paneled doors of Lucy Fry's sitting room look exactly as they might have done when first installed, proving that the designs of the period have an elegance and beauty that will never fade.

Right: A beautiful nineteenth-century Windsor chair sits comfortably by a small writing desk.

Left and right: The
heavy proportions
of this fireplace
are softened by an
eclectic collection of
treasures that makes
up an intriguing
display. The old cotton
reel, a crisp dried leaf,
and scallop shells
adorning the tops of
picture frames are, in
their own way, as
valuable and as
beautiful as the
antique Staffordshire
figurines and, treated
with the same respect,
contribute just as much
character to a room.

So, allow your decorating scheme to evolve around the house. Exposed wooden beams and stone flags on the floors? Play up the rough, rustic charm. Elegantly proportioned, high-ceilinged rooms? Make the most of them by emphasizing the feeling of light and space. Wide window ledges backed by small leaded panes of glass? Enhance the feeling of coziness by filling them with hotchpotch collections of treasures that you've picked up over the years.

Some periods have had a greater impact on interior design than others: Colonial style, for example, is typified by its simplicity and almost classically perfect proportions, while the Arts & Crafts movement of the 1880s and 1890s valued beauty and craftsmanship as highly as function. But even if your home is modern in design, you can still decide which elements of a particular style appeal to you and try to recreate something of the same atmosphere by installing reclaimed, original materials and artifacts from the period.

Above: Books share their space with a pair of reproduction china dogs, a display case of birds' eggs, and an old, cracked china mug.

Right: A vintage sailing boat, a jardinière filled with silver baubles and ostrich eggs, and a group of antique decanters—a motley collection—fills the space beautifully.

Objects from a similar period tend to look good together, even when they're made from very different materials, and this is one way of unifying the look of a room. The objects don't even need to have a common theme—bucolic eighteenth-century shepherdesses will sit happily alongside silver snuff boxes, ancient fossils next to a pair of nineteenth-century firedogs, or an early Mickey Mouse figure in the company of an old wind-up gramophone.

However, it's a mistake to carry authenticity to extremes and get rid of things that you love just because they come from different periods. Shape, color, and size (and effective contrasts of all three) are all design elements that you can use to create attractive-looking collections of objects dating from very different periods. Mixing and matching is at the very heart of vintage style; it's what enables you to create interiors that are a reflection of you, your lifestyle, and your passions.

Left: Artist Lucy Fry has a brilliant talent to amuse by adding incongruous details. This classical marble bust, with his mop of curly hair and laughing expression, ridicules the elegant design of the mantlepiece in her dining room. A swag of dried hops picked from a nearby field is draped along the mantel, harking back to (and, at the same time, poking fun at) the classical penchant for adornment in the form of flowing vines.

classical details

Classical details such as statues might seem a little incongruous in a domestic interior at first glance, but they hark back to the heydays of the so-called Grand Tour in the eighteenth and nineteenth centuries, when it was common practice for the wealthy to tour the major cities of Europe to further their education. Although few of us can afford genuine Ancient Greek or Roman artifacts (and even if we could, there's a strong argument in favor of keeping such objects in museums, where they can be enjoyed by everyone), good-quality reproductions are readily available at reasonable cost. One or two large pieces in the right kind of setting can have huge dramatic impact.

Scale is the key here: marble statues, busts, and the like need to be big enough to make their presence felt, but not so huge that they dominate and overpower everything else. At the other extreme, lots of small objects can make a room look very bitty and unified. If you're planning to use such items in your own home, think very carefully about exactly where you're going to locate them. Moreover, the dividing line between classical and kitsch can sometimes be a very fine one! My advice would be to make sure that you stand firmly on either one side or the other—and remember that a little humor in interior design rarely goes awry.

Clean white floorboards are a delicious starting point from which to approach the decoration of a room as, like an artist's blank canvas or a simple white shirt that you can dress up or dress down, they leave the way free for any kind of treatment. The character of the room will be created by the furnishings. Although white floorboards seem to work particularly well with the elegantly proportioned eighteenth-century neo-classical style, you could develop the room in virtually any direction you choose, including simple rustic style. Restraint is essential, however: take care not to lose the lovely light and airy feel that you started with.

Right: A reproduction-Louis-XV bergère armchair is framed by vintage curtains. The ornate table might be overpowering without its coat of white paint.

Below: An antique chinoiserie chest that stands near a delicately carved sofa with a simple vintage ticking cushion, and a small campaign stool.

christmas spirit

Nothing makes me feel more snug and secure than a roaring log fire. In fact, one of my biggest luxuries is to have a log fire burning all day long in the winter; the scent of woodsmoke in the morning reminds me of happy hours spent roasting chestnuts after long country walks through the frost and snow.

I, for one, can see no reason for not making every day of the winter as cozy and festive as Christmas—and if you're lucky enough to have a working fireplace, then you're already well on the way. The trick is to embellish what you've already got by adding a few extra touches, such as fairy lights strung along the mantelpiece and chunky hand-knitted socks hanging up by the fire.

Rich reds and browns, contrasting with dark greens, are good colors for a cozy atmosphere. We associate all these with traditional Christmas decorations—perhaps because they were popular in Victorian times, when many of our Christmas traditions first originated.

Left: This dark and cozy library is lit only by the fire and the fairy lights, like something out of a Victorian Christmas tableau.

Above left: Hand-knitted socks are worn underneath a red flannel petticoat.

Above right: Old leather-bound books share shelf space with a lusterware mug, a vintage Welsh bowl, and a pair of simple boats in wooden frames. The rich, dark colors are ideally suited to evoking the spirit of Christmas.

Many people are scared of using dark colors in small dark rooms, but I have always advocated treating a small, dark room as just that. There is little point in trying to make it lighter by painting it white: it will merely look like a small, dark room that has had a coat of white paint. Go the whole hog and paint it in rich, warm colors, and counteract the darkness by paying particular attention to the lighting. Lamps strategically placed in corners and on tables will not detract from its coziness, but will provide intimate pools of light in which you can lose yourself with a good book or your thoughts. Fairy lights need not be restricted to the Christmas tree: draped along mantelpieces and shelf edges, they will add glitter and glamor and that all-essential party atmosphere. Night lights and candles are lovely ways of creating a romantic atmosphere (try metal candle sconces on the walls for an authentic "olde worlde" feeling) and candles scented with wintry spices such as cinnamon and cloves conjure up images of mulled wine and Christmas cake.

Above left: Children's shoes lighten the grandeur of the gilt lampstand and pictures in a corner of this living room.

Above right: Festive fairy lights surround a gilt mirror flanked by giant candlesticks, while the line of roses somehow makes the whole scene more homey and personal.

happy accidents

It is unexpected juxtapositions of objects and ideas and, above all, a spirit of playfulness on the part of the owner or designer that really bring a room to life. As a designer, I find it's quite liberating to take an object that, superficially at least, appears very grand (a huge gilt mirror, for example, or an ornate vase) and deliberately try to make it less pompous by placing it next to something very frivolous or something that has great sentimental value, such as baby shoes or a child's teddy bear.

Above left: Richly colored fabrics—an antique French linen sheet, a red and white quilt, a plaid-covered book, and a kilim-covered cushion—create warmth and atmosphere in this cozy study.

Above right: Cloth- and leather-bound books, mixed with china and fabric-covered storage boxes, make these library shelves more homey.

Interior decorator Pia MacLean has done this to perfection in her home, as the photographs on these two pages demonstrate. Intimate little still-life corners like this, mixing sizes and shapes, colors and periods, are an inspiration to all budding collectors of vintage and demonstrate, if proof is needed, that vintage living is about pleasing the senses, not about conforming to pre-conceived ideas about what works and what doesn't.

I find that some of the most appealing corners of my own home have come about quite by chance as I've experimented with different combinations and this, for me, is a large part of the charm of vintage living. You can never sit back and say that a room is complete. It evolves and develops, just as you do—and that's the perfect excuse to visit yet another fleamarket or thrift store!

vintage bedrooms

Vintage looks well in a bedroom, be it an old quilt thrown over the bed, or worn and faded floral curtains, which might have seen better days, allowing splinters of daylight through their diminishing threads. Piles of vintage cushions scattered on the bed, treasured family photographs, or carefully chosen china in which to display sumptuous arrangements of cottage-garden flowers can all combine to create comfortable havens where you can relax and feel totally at ease. Create your own dream combination from the reds and pinks of crushed summer fruits, rose petals, four-poster beds, and drapes of floating muslin. The following pages are an eclectic and inspirational collection of different vintage bedroom styles.

Above: A scrap of vintage toile de jouy fabric finds a new lease of life as a lampshade cover. Easy to make, it is captivating in its simplicity.

Right: This four-poster bed, from a collection by Lena Proudlock, is based on a simple Swedish design of her forebears. The plump lines of the antique linen and the striking stripes of the quilt add warmth to the pure white room.

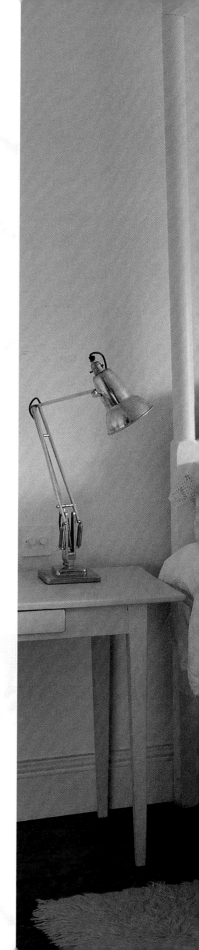

fabric flair

Regardless of whether your personal taste in bed linen veers toward crisp cotton sheets topped by warm woollen blankets, modern duvet covers, or cozy vintage quilts and eiderdowns, fabric plays an essential decorative (and functional) role in any bedroom. Fabrics can immediately soften harsh lines, introduce color, and give the whole room a much more feminine feel.

Although we tend to think of vintage style as being very pretty and predominantly floral, there's no reason why you shouldn't use solid colors, too. In fact, there's a sound historical precedent as, in both the United States and Great Britain, there's a well-established tradition of quilts made in bold, wide stripes in just two colors— the Bars quilts of the Amish and the so-called "strippy" quilts of Wales and the north of England. This type of bed linen can look extremely effective in a very simple room painted white, as it instantly gives tremendous graphic impact, warmth, and color.

Left: Reproduction fabrics give a room that authentic vintage feel. Here, the checked bed canopy is a copy of an 1835 fabric woven in Périgord (southwest France) and reproduced in nine colors by London designer Nicole Fabre. The curtains are made from Cabbages & Roses canvas.

Right: Hand printed French antique linen sheets were made into curtains and the bedroom chair covered in an embroidered linen sheet. The vintage ticking, and floral cushions, and the fine gauze mosquito net add an air of luxury.

Many people are scared of mixing lots of different fabric patterns in the same room, but, to me, few things are more bland and uninspiring than rooms in which every scrap of fabric, from the curtains to small details like lampshades, is the same design. Coordination is all very well, but when it's carried to extremes it ceases to have any decorative impact. You can happily mix checks and stripes with floral prints and solid colors, provided you bear in mind two things: the relative sizes of the fabric patterns, and the color ways.

In terms of scale, I find it's best to go for one quite large, bold pattern as the main fabric—this could be a chintz-inspired floral or a strong check—and balance it with smaller patterns (perhaps sprigs or narrow stripes). A very wide stripe would fight with a bit-patterned floral design, as they would compete for attention.

When it comes to color, again, decide first on your main theme and balance other elements with it. You might decide to go for strong contrasts (red and green, for example), or to opt for toning colors (perhaps various shades of pink or soft pastel shades as in the vintage quilt shown opposite). Instinct is your best guide, but to get an idea of how your scheme will look, take samples of the fabrics you're thinking of using, scatter them randomly on the floor or bed, and move them around without consciously trying to decide what goes with what: this makes it easier to see if there are any potential clashes.

Below left: This gorgeous quilt dates from the nineteenth century and was made gathering circles of fabric around pennies.

Below right: Flowers in toning shades impart a sense of unity to any decorating scheme.

Right: The quilt and vintage pillowslips are made from very different patterns of fabric, but the fact that they date from the same period helps to create a feeling of coherence.

Made as Curtains also

elegant restraint

ood interior design is about maintaining a sense of balance and it is perfectly possible, through the use of a few well-chosen objects, to create a room that is neither cluttered nor minimalist but still very much vintage in style.

A feeling of light and space is all important in interiors like this, and it is a good idea to establish that feeling at the outset. Pale-colored walls and floors, and sheer fabrics draped at the windows, provide an ethereal-looking framework around which you can build the rest of the design.

The furniture comes next and it is vital not to cram in too much—a few key pieces, positioned with regard to the symmetry of the room, are generally sufficient.

Left: In Pia Maclean's bedroom, the purest of white is punctuated with touches of pale blues.

Above left: A terracotta pot full of lavender picks up the blue tones of the eighteenth-century French daybed and its ticking cover.

Above right: A favorite floral shirt hangs on the door of the roughly painted closet and introduces a soft, feminine color.

After the furniture, bed linen and curtains are probably the most important design elements of any bedroom, as they can both be considered part of the overall framework and feel of the room. This is your chance to start playing with color and pattern, and what you choose will depend very much on the mood you want to establish. Stripes might be a good choice for a symmetrical, eighteenth-century room; on their own they can be used to give a room a formal feel. Floral prints, on the other hand, tend to evoke a softer, more romantic atmosphere. And, of course, every combination of color, pattern, and even fabric type, will have a different effect. Decide what mood you want to create, and then experiment with fabric swatches, colors, and patterns to see what works best.

Above: Pia Maclean has managed to create the perfect balance in this room—a peaceful haven of comfort and a room of great beauty that still contains enough to distract and please the eye.

Last, but by no means least, comes the fun part—the decoration and choice of embellishments. Be careful not to overdo it. It's very easy to fall in love with certain pieces and feel that you have to include them, but, if you have too many, the whole visual balance that you've striven so hard to create will be destroyed. It's much better to have a few medium- to large-scale decorative pieces than lots of small ones that make no visual impact in big, near-empty spaces. Rather than trying to fill every corner of the room with things of interest, restrict yourself to a few cleverly positioned vignettes: whether they're made up of personal possessions, quirky collections of unrelated objects, or simply things of beauty that it's a delight to wake up to in the morning, these are what will give the room character and its own inimitable sense of style.

Above left: A cherrywood bateau lit found in a junk shop sits majestically in a corner of Katie Forman's spare bedroom.

Above right: A few carefully chosen details—a ribbon-trimmed lampshade and large-bloomed roses in front of a gilt mirror—are enough to create a delightfully feminine vignette in just one small corner.

Right: Formal symmetry and soft romanticism combine to perfection in this room. A curious mix of grandiose and homey, the key to success in rooms like this is knowing exactly when to stop.

Vintage furniture has so much more character than modern and, thankfully, there are still rich pickings to be had all over the world: thrift stores, fleamarkets, auction rooms, and garage sales are the most luscious words in the English language to a collector of vintage. It may take you several attempts to find the piece of your dreams, but persevere: it's impossible to predict what will come up for sale and you never know when it will be your lucky day. Equally, it's a mistake to go to a sale with too precise an idea in your mind of what you want to find. Be spontaneous, go with the flow, and you won't be disappointed.

Right: A ravishing attic bedroom, its whiteness is enough to hold one spellbound. Although lovers of vintage have a need for clutter, piles of vintage fabrics, and one-off pieces of kitsch in their lives, the spiritual calm in this near-empty room makes my anti-minimalist philosophy vanish into thin air.

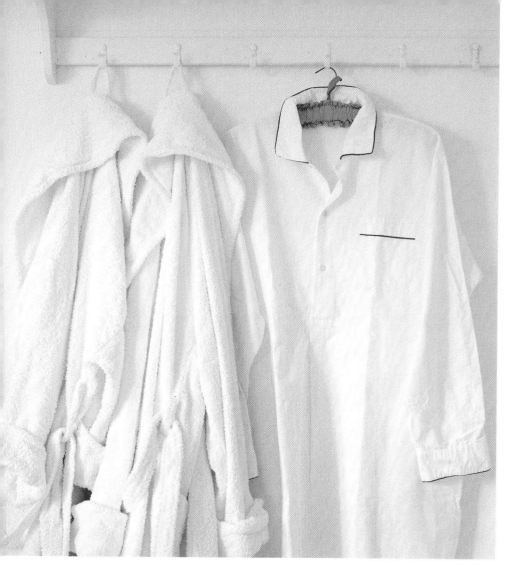

Above left: Crisply laundered nightclothes decorate the wall of this pure white bedroom

Above right: A simple arrangement of tall delphiniums and scabious echoes the colors of the antique linen used to cover the charmingly shaped bedroom chair. On the perfectly proportioned eighteenth-century sash window, nineteenth-century glass paperweights glint in the sun.

flowers in the bedroom

There is nothing quite so evocative as the sight of faded, old-fashioned roses—either in their natural state or captured indelibly on a piece of fabric. It is inconceivable that roses will ever suffer the indignity of being unfashionable—poppies perhaps, and sunflowers may come and go, but roses? Never.

Above: Cabbages & Roses "Hatley" print on Irish linen blinds: its faded gentleness is delicate and unassuming.

People sometimes feel that flowers are out of place in a bedroom, perhaps fearing that they'll make the room too feminine for the man of the house. True, they do soften a room but they also bring it to life—and to me, no room is complete without flowers in some shape or form. Cottage garden flowers—roses, peonies, delphiniums, and the like—complement vintage style beautifully. Massed together in simple containers, their colors are soft and muted just like those of faded vintage fabrics, their heady perfumes bring a natural air of romance that suits bedrooms to perfection.

Above: This is a captivating window seat, built into a beautiful eighteenth-century bay window in the country home of artist Tony Fry and his wife Sabrina. The faded floral curtains frame the space without detracting from it.

Right: Light streams into this London bedroom belonging to painter Anthea Craigmyle. Her unfailing eye for color and ability to find the perfect piece of furniture make her homes as inspiring as her paintings.

quiet corners

Bedrooms should be sanctuaries where you can hide away from the world and snatch a few precious moments on your own, as well as places where you go to sleep. Even if space is limited, it's usually possible to create a small area within a bedroom for just that purpose. A small bedroom chair, preferably one with soft curves, and perhaps a side table or corner of a dressing table where you can keep a book, or a notebook, a few treasured family photographs, and trinkets are all you need. A window seat where you can watch the world go by is a bonus.

No matter how formal the furnishings and décor, a bedroom should still have a homey, lived-in feel. Think of the blandness of hotel bedrooms where, if you're lucky, there may be a few mass-produced prints on the walls to liven up the décor: no one wants to create that kind of feeling in their own home. However, a single small, glass-fronted cupboard will allow you to set out a few treasured possessions and immediately stamp your personality on the room.

Left: A simple, painted display cupboard made around 1900, houses a collection of seashells and treasured finds. Although it takes up very little space, it instantly stamps the personality and interests of the owner on the room.

Right: Katie Forman's charming desk is cluttered with a harmonious array. The wall cupboard above it is lined with vintage-style fabrics by designer Cath Kidston, providing a visual link with the soft furnishings in the rest of the room.

You don't even need space for a whole cupboard: you can create small areas of color and interest with nothing more than a single shelf above a radiator, or a tiny corner of a dressing table. Hang knick-knacks such as embroidered purses or Shaker-style hearts from drawer and door handles, tuck small postcards into the edges of picture frames, cover storage boxes in pretty fabrics or paper and use them to house love letters or photos: but make a conscious effort to make your mark.

Above left. A Venetian writing desk is transformed into a delicate and feminine-looking piece of furniture by the addition of a coat or two of white paint. The curtains, made from cream-colored grosgrain, drape elegantly because of their weight.

Above right: A newly painted chest of drawers and bedstead originate from the late Victorian era.

Mahogany and other dark woods may have been popular with the Victorians, but they seem rather too heavy for today's interiors. However, it takes nothing more than a coat or two of white paint to transform them into elegant pieces of furniture that would grace any room. Immediately the darkness disappears, and the beauty of their shape is laid bare for all to see—worth bearing in mind if you've inherited somber but well-made pieces that you would feel guilty about getting rid of.

White-painted wooden furniture is almost always a good bet in vintage style. Not only does it lighten the mood of a room, but it also provides you with a neutral backdrop on which to set out all those lovely ornaments and flowers, books and bric-a-brac.

Right: Built-in cupboards, in the home of Clare Faull, have chicken wire panels lined with a clever mixture of floral and checked fabrics. The tiny vintage hand-embroidered bag is from an extensive collection —such delightful decorative objects cry out to be displayed in full view rather than stored out of sight.

bathtime bliss

Bathrooms, as well as being obviously functional, should be treated as sanctuaries in which you can laze in self-indulgent luxury, and one of the greatest luxuries in life is to own a bathroom large enough to accommodate furniture—an armchair, a table full of fragrant unguents, a freestanding towel rail. The second greatest luxury is a working fireplace: I can think of nothing more delicious than sinking into soapy suds in a room lit by candles and the flickering flames of a wood fire. When the fire is not in use, place a generously sized vase of fresh flowers on the hearth.

Left and below: These two bathrooms, so diametrically opposed in style, are equally inviting. The tiny cottage bathroom, left, is furnished with freestanding bathroom furniture—a washstand for storing soaps, and an antiquated commode, now serving as a chair. In the graceful yet understated bathroom below, light streams through the vintage lace of the curtains.

Above: An enameled tin cup serves as a vase, and a child's 1930s' tin bucket holds a collection of family toothbrushes in this seaside bathroom. Seashells always look beautiful wherever they may fetch up!

Left: This beautiful Edwardian bathtub once suffered the ignominy of being used as a cattle trough! Now it is restored to its original glory and function in the home of nurse Clare Faull.

When space allows, a freestanding bathtub is the ultimate luxury, and if you can find a reclaimed Victorian or other antique bath, which were often beautifully made with elegantly cast feet, then you can wallow in sweet-scented luxury to your heart's content. One of the delights of antique bathtubs is their great depth; because of the need to save energy, bathtubs today tend to be much shallower.

Although people often include seashells and other seaside souvenirs in bathrooms, don't restrict yourself to water-related themes. Antique salerooms and junk stores often have old advertisements for sale and you can pick up charming adverts for soaps and cosmetics at very reasonable prices. Use vintage china bowls to house hand-made soaps and other bathtime essentials: edge towels with strips of pretty vintage fabrics; decant shower gels and bath foams into elegantly shaped glass bottles and display them on the window ledge so that the light shines through, creating a stained-glass effect: with a little thought, bathrooms can be every bit as pretty and romantic as any other room in the house.

Above: An ancient and much-loved teddy, dressed to match Cath Kidston's vintage reproduction bedclothes, looks perfectly at home.

Right: In a cozy bedroom at the top of the house, the fairy lights create a magical atmosphere.

junior vintage

The notion of rooms specifically designed for children is relatively new: it was the Victorians who gave us the quintessential nursery, along with the idea that toys were made to educate and not simply to amuse. The Victorians' idolization of childhood was the incentive for the emergence of a huge range of mass-produced toys. Dolls' houses, toy soldiers, sailing boats—all miniature versions of adult life—provided scope for tiny fingers and young minds to create their own imaginary worlds, while mechanical games and globes fostered their curiosity about the world around them. Long after their original owners have grown up and had children (and even grandchildren) of their own, these vintage toys and books remain to decorate rooms, waiting to amuse the next generation.

*A veritable menagerie of
creatures old and new, is
lined up on a vivid pink
nursery sofa.*

Above: An inviting jumble of toys and books in the nursery belongs to Katie Forman's children. Happily, reproductions of many Victorian games and toys, such as the toy theatre and hobby horse, are available today.

Right: A beautiful old rocking horse that has delighted many generations of children, sits in an attic bedroom. A Victorian decoupage screen provides the perfect backdrop.

There is no doubt that the playthings that our forebears' children enjoyed have an enduring beauty that their present-day counterparts lack. In those days, toys, along with so much else, were made to last and a great deal of care and attention to detail went into making them objects to be treasured. There is something truly magical about passing them down through the generations for others to share. I have always believed that any object that has been much loved and cared for absorbs a certain atmosphere. If you are not fortunate enough to have inherited such vintage playthings, however, there is, luckily, a wealth of children's paraphernalia on sale in antique stores and salerooms. They make perfect decorations for children's bedrooms and nurseries, as well as being a rather more wholesome distraction than the brightly colored plastic toys of today.

Above: Dressing-up clothes mingle with works of children's art at the entrance from the nursery to the kitchen.

Right: Maudie Buchanan's bedroom, is an enchanting jumble of childhood paraphernalia.

Children need to be in environments where their minds are stimulated and challenged, and it is essential to provide them with playthings that stretch their imagination. Dressing-up boxes should be a feature of all children's bedrooms and nurseries, in my view: a few old clothes, hats and scarves, costume jewelry and badges are all they need to lose themselves in their own imaginary world, and fleamarkets and jumble sales are great places to pick up clothes and accessories at very little cost.

Art is another area that ought to be developed and your child's first colored-pencil scribbles, however unrecognizable they seem, are things that you will treasure for ever more. Give them all the encouragement you can by devoting a special area of the home to their art, even if you simply make a "gallery" by taping their drawings to the back of their bedroom door. It will improve their self-confidence no end and give you immeasurable pleasure, as well as an insight into the way that they see themselves and their lives.

Whenever possible, try to involve your children in any decisions about how their rooms should be decorated. It's important for them that they have a space that they can call their own, where no grown-ups interfere, and involving them in the decision-making process will make them feel that the room is truly theirs.

Of course, it's easier with very young children: you're on fairly safe ground with dinosaurs and enchanted forests, or cuddly animals and fairytale castles. When they're a little bit older, things get more complicated. Children's enthusiasms come and go like the changing tides: no point in decorating their room like something out of Hogwarts School of Witchcraft and Wizardry if you know that in three or six months' time they'll decry the whole thing as being childish beyond belief and demand something new. My advice is to opt for generic settings—star-studded skies or a colorful landscape in which they can invent their own stories—rather than anything that's specific to their latest passion. The décor will not only last for longer, but it will also give their imaginations more scope as it's not linked to any one story line. And make the most of it while you can: children grow up before you can blink and it won't be long before they're plotting to paint the ceiling black and putting "Keep Out" signs on the door.

Right: In a cozy bedroom belonging to Clare Faull's children, teddies wear re-cycled Fair Isle cardigans completing this picture of a vintage childhood.

Above: An old painted stepladder is used as bedside shelves—home to a dog named "Dog," Fair Isle blankets, books, and photographs.

For quick and easy changes, however, you can't beat simply making a new duvet cover or adding a wallpaper border. Both these things can be done in the course of an afternoon. If the rest of the décor is fairly neutral, then this has an immediate impact. As the photographs on these two pages show, children's rooms don't have to be decorated in bright colors with cartoon characters and up-to-the-minute gadgetry: they can be stimulating without sending your child into hyperactive overdrive, calm without being soporific.

Above: A corner of Anthea Craigmyle's sitting room is reserved for visiting children.

Your children themselves may turn out to be vintage stylists in the making. Most children have something that they feel passionate about, whether it's ballet or baseball, cats or cars. Encourage them to build up their own collections and perhaps even come with you to markets and sales to see what they can find. You'll be opening their eyes not only to the pleasures of collecting, but also to the fact that interior decorating is about making spaces work for you —and it's fun.

retreats & hideaways

Everyone needs a place where they can relax and escape from the pressures of everyday life for a few precious moments—and there's no reason why those places shouldn't be every bit as cozy and comforting and filled with lovely things as the rest of your home. This chapter looks at ways of creating and decorating those special retreats in your life, whether they're a permanent part of your home or temporary hideaways that you visit only occasionally.

The very word "retreat" conjures up, in my mind at least, a vision of a rural idyll, removed from the hustle and bustle of normal life, and if you have even the tiniest garden or back yard you can create the same atmosphere without having to move far from your front door. A veranda, or a small area of decking or paving over which you can erect a tentlike covering in bad weather, will provide a kind of extra room with the benefit of access to the open air. Cherish every moment that you can spend outdoors—but make your retreat a real home from home with comfortable seating, plants and flowers, decorative lamps or candles, and of course, books and games to allow you to while away the hours.

Above: Ancient and well-used terra-cotta pots slide gently into the landscape of any vintage surrounding, and the lovely crinkly leaves and bright flowers of geraniums are undemanding and easy on the eye.

Left: The back wall of Brigette Buchanan's veranda, decorated in much the same way as an interior wall, has a collection of vintage games, toys, and colorful paper lanterns.

Right: The wrought-iron staircase, painted white, is used more for displaying flowers than for gaining access to the upstairs room.

Above: A charming basket is, here kitted out with a vintage blanket, cool drinks, and books—everything you need for a day on the beach.

Left: A picnic by the sea is complete with an array of pretty towels, a picnic basket, and a gingham cushion.

days out

Comfort and good food being at all times upmost on my agenda, nothing gives me greater pleasure than packing a picnic in a vintage wicker basket and heading off for a day in the country or by the sea with cushions, pretty towels and, most importantly, a sturdy beach rug. My version features newly developed printed floral oilcloth on one side, while on the other traditional white toweling comes complete with a pocket for stowing away car keys and seashells collected from the beach—all I need in the way of creature comforts. Food always seems to taste better in the open air, and simple snacks of freshly baked bread and cakes, with perhaps some cheese and tomatoes newly picked from the garden, make my happiness complete.

Left: In the Strutt children's tree house, the furnishings are taken every bit as seriously as in a normal house!

Right: Ned and Tom Barton's railway carriage bedroom has custom-made beds and an antique gauze pelmet.

occasional hideaways

When our children were younger, we built a tree house in the garden for them which proved to be the perfect little hideaway. Beds were installed, curtains made from scraps of fabric sewn to bamboo canes, and the house filled with books, toys and other treasures, crockery and cutlery, and all the things one needs in a real home. The children spent hours there, shopping, cleaning, rearranging the furniture, building benches and wooden boats, and making camp fires to cook their breakfast on. They were close enough for us to be able to keep an eye on them, but it was their space: they could do what they wanted and were blissfully happy. A simpler and less permanent hideaway is the canvas tent shown on pages 28–31, ideal as a play area in which your children can grow in both stature and maturity.

Grown-ups need to get away from it all, too, and I suppose our equivalent of a tree house or a makeshift tent in the garden, if we're lucky enough to be able to afford it, is a weekend cottage or vacation home. Even though we don't live there full time, we still want to make it somewhere that is undeniably ours and contains our furniture and possessions rather than the cast-off fixtures and fittings that seem to fill so much rented vacation accommodation. And that, I think, is the key to creating a comfortable retreat. It might be tempting to furnish it with things you no longer need or want in your permanent home in order to save money—slightly rickety furniture or crockery that you don't really like any more, for example—but if you want to make it a real home from home, then you need to decorate it with the same care and attention to detail that you would use in any other area of your life. Surround yourself with familiar and well-loved objects and you'll feel at ease every time you walk through the door.

But retreats are a form of escapism, too, and give you an opportunity to indulge in decorative whims and fancies that you might not want to live with all the time. Let your imagination run wild: perhaps use colors that you wouldn't normally choose, and fill it with quirky decorations that bring out the frivolous side of your nature.

This railway-carriage beach house belongs to the Barton family.

Far left: The wood-paneled bathroom is screened with muslin curtains.

Left: Lily Barton's bedroom has vintage-style brass beds dressed in 1950s spotted and cowboy-patterned bedlinen.

Right: In the master bedroom, the mosquito net and formal bed hangings add stature to an otherwise simple room.

Left: Many of the
original railway-
carriage fittings have
been retained,
including the leather
straps for opening and
closing windows, and
the etched glass
panes.

Right: Tablecloth
weights in the shape
of animals are a
quirky but functional
decorative detail.

Far right: The dining
area is divided from
the rest of the house
by curtains.

My philosophy when it comes to vacation homes is quite simple: dare to be different! You might not want to live on a houseboat, or in a railway carriage, or in a beach hut all year round, but such dwellings have a wonderfully individual character and you can emphasize this in your choice of decoration.

This is precisely what the Barton family has done with the railway-carriage beach house shown here and on the previous two pages. Built by joining two vintage railway carriages together, painted in subtle tones throughout, and furnished with simple and well-designed fittings, every inch has been meticulously planned and the bedrooms decorated to suit the age and sex of the occupants. However, as you can see, the house still retains much of a railway-carriage feel with its original brass door fittings, "No Smoking" signs etched into the glass of the windows, and the occasional 1930s' brass plaque instructing passengers to "Please refrain from spitting." The result is a playful yet infinitely inviting retreat that all the family can enjoy.

storage and screening

Practicality rears its ugly head in even the most romantic and dreamlike of retreats with the question of where on earth do you store all those things that you've brought with you? One needs so much more paraphernalia in the country than in urban life, and all this additional clutter needs to be housed. Food shopping alone can be a major chore, as the distance you need to travel to buy something as simple and essential as a pint of milk make it both prohibitively expensive and time-consuming to pop out to buy a single item. So, large larders are a must and should, if possible, be built on a north-facing wall. Using slate on the bottom shelf is a practical and cool alternative to wood.

Clothes and boots are the next problem. If you haven't got adequate cupboard space you can live out of a suitcase for a while—but muddy boots and wet coats do need to stored somewhere and boots, in particular, seem to take up a lot of space. A porch is ideal, as is simple home-made storage such as that shown below.

Left: This home-made boot rack, made from wooden broom handles fixed at an angle onto 6-in. (15-cm) pieces of wood, is an ingenious and simple storage solution.

Right: This is the tree house in which my children have spent many happy hours. The simple, unhemmed curtain helps to screen the inhabitants from the adult world.

Left: A riding jacket is stowed on a nail in the wall of the tree house.

Shirts and jackets can be put on hangers and hung on hooks or nails or over door handles, providing instant decoration as well as easy access, and laundry bags are invaluable for storing dirty clothes. Large drawstring bags are simple to make from canvas or reasonably heavy fabric; they pack flat, so you can bring several with you without worrying about how much space they'll take up, and look decorative as well as functional.

Ideally, your rural retreat will be so isolated or well-screened by trees that you'd have no need of curtains for extra privacy—and what a joy to wake up every morning to the dawn chorus and the sun streaming through your window. Back in the real world, however, most of us need to ensure we have a certain amount of privacy.

When it comes to putting up curtains, the lovely thing about decorating a tree house, or other occasional hideaway that it used more as a play area than as a real home, is the amount of instant decorating that you can get away with. How lovely life would be if one could change the curtains in a room with no more than an unhemmed piece of fabric, a bamboo cane, and a staple gun. This is how I solved the curtain problem in our tree house—so simple a child could do it!

Very formal window treatments go against the whole spirit of retreats and hideaways, but, for more permanent residences, adopt the same quick and easy approach I used in my tree house: simply turn over the top of a piece of fabric twice and stitch to make a channel through which you can thread a metal rod or a cane as a curtain pole. And remember that a retreat is precisely that: a chance to recharge your batteries and unwind, and *not* a decorating endurance test!

Just as we thought that the photography for this book was at an end, we noticed from an upstairs window in the Fry's house the delectable pile of old terra-cotta pots shown far right. Somehow they seem to sum up my philosophy for both life and work. There is a gentle beauty in unassuming, everyday objects, things that have been passed down from generation to generation. They have not been artistically positioned by a professional stylist and yet their arrangement is so unselfconscious and pleasing to the eye that we couldn't resist photographing them. They are not fashionable objects of desire, new and cutting edge, today's "must-have" status symbol. Take them or leave them, they are what they are.

Above: Even humble edifices passed down from a previous generation have a certain beauty that seems to be lacking in the modern equivalent. This greenhouse, which has served the Fry family for many years, nestles unassumingly among the ferns

Right: Terra-cotta plant pots are so much a part of the garden that one almost feels they have grown there.

CHAPTER SIX

creating vintage style

Decorating your home in the vintage style is an organic process, as rewarding and enjoyable as living in the finished rooms. Touring the flea markets, discovering ingenious ways to re-use old pieces, developing your individual passions, and reveling in the joys of a bargain, are the only skills you need.

kitchens: china and glass

As with much that is vintage, creating collections for your home is a gentle, gradual process that develops over time. China and glass are they keynotes of the kitchen, not least because these collections, unlike those of many other styles, are designed to be both beautiful and constantly in use. Achieve the look by simply picking the individual pieces you love; a single plate or glass, even a much-loved and chipped remnant will also work well, then purposely mismatch them with other pieces. Although you should switch off the desire to co-ordinate things, you can theme your collection in many ways. Theming by color makes immediate impact; cream and white, for instance, add a cool, fresh look to every space. You could also choose to collect

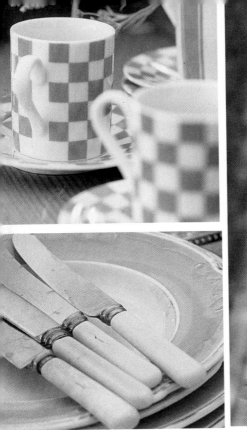

pieces from the same period. As you acquire pieces, contrast textures and shades in the collection; match the translucent finish of a porcelain tea cup, for instance, with the rough glaze of a stoneware milk jug, or a simple terra-cotta bowl with some fine engraved glass for a more adventurous look. True vintage finishes include creamware, majolica, European porcelain manufacturers such as Royal Worcester and Wedgewood, and less expensive Czech and Eastern European makes, while vintage metal and plastic include tin and Bakelite homeware. Pieces of china and sets of glassware are still available at surprisingly low cost from markets and thrift stores; bear in mind that, ideal for the true vintage hunter, prices are much lower for semi-complete dinner services and for worn pieces from old country kitchens. As china and glass are fragile, and hard to transport, the dealers are usually receptive to bargaining. If you intend to use your finds purely for decoration, the odd crack or chip only adds to its intrinsic beauty. But do be aware that condition of the china and glass is important if it is to be used every day—check for cracks in handles and lips as damaged cups, jugs, and particularly glasses, are not suitable.

Above left: This eclectic assembly of ornaments, is created from majolica figures, mixed with seashells, cotton reels and dried leaves.

Above right: Draw attention to your finest pieces with grouping; here, a gilded carved lampstand is enhanced with gold accents from the picture frames.

I f you have a motley collection of ornaments in your home, make the most of their different styles and shapes with an exuberant set of vintage displays. Taken too seriously, a home can all too easily become a museum, with an invitation to view but not touch. Start with valuable, family, or inherited pieces, which you want to show off, and be adventurous—pair a grand lampstand with a surprising or eccentric item such as a pair of tiny child's shoes, as seen above, and add an element of humour to create a relaxed living room. As you display pieces, the key rule is to follow your own individuality; if you have a passion for sea shells or tin buckets, shoes,

Above left: An all white collection will suit most rooms, and provides a modern contrast to other vintage displays.

Above center: Large bows on a cushion soften the formality of the living room;

Above right: Using valuable family pieces in casual settings relaxes a living room.

ships or sealing wax, be assured that if you love it, so will others. Do collect artifacts that were not designed as ornaments but are nonetheless lovely. Pieces that represent a moment of family history, such as your daughter's first party dress, for instance, will look delightful as a drape hanging over a small corner window. To achieve atmosphere, coziness, and warmth, display items that are personal to you—bought or inherited and assembled in a way unique to you and your family. When browsing the markets and thrift shops, allow your visual senses to take over. In the living room, beauty and charm are all; if something attracts your eye for no reason of practicality or good sense, it may well be the very piece that will enhance your life and home for many years to come.

Opposite: Color coordinate antique and reproduction fabrics for an eclectic but elegant look: (above) a mix of flora and toile de jouy, (below) a riot of florals.

Left and above: Two old wing armchairs, each playing the same role, but in utterly different guises for summer and winter; above, swathed in an antique white linen sheet for freshness in warm weather, while, left, plaid dress fabric creates a cozy winter spot.

living rooms: fabrics

The finest and most suitable vintage fabrics to use are those that are already worn and faded, but are nonetheless durable enough to withstand more years of family wear and tear. Made from all-natural materials, many traditional fabrics were extremely well made, and those that survive well include velvets, woven wool worsted or plaid, linen, and tapestry. Silk, although beautiful, ages fast in the sun, and should be used well away from a window. When choosing your living room decor, place your largest pieces first; a unique sofa throw, for instance, could be paired with deliberately mismatched cushions, which you can create as patchwork from other favorite, but smaller, scraps of less durable materials. The nature of vintage style means that most of your pieces will be unique. Therefore do not feel constrained to co-ordinate your room strictly. Be inspired by other cultures too; an antique Turkish cushion, above opposite, provides a lush contrast with a simple old French linen sheet. Sun-fading and visible patching are part of the appeal, but, if you seek perfection, take your pick from the bouquets of authentic reproduction floral prints and even from historical textile collections.

bedrooms: fabrics

Happily there are many rich pickings in flea markets and thrift stores, and, typical of vintage style, the inexpensive furnishing of your bedroom can be an immense pleasure. The more traditional natural fabrics are ideal here; choose cottons, washed- or brushed- cotton blankets, real feather comforters and old linen, which is particularly durable. Bear in mind the rules for using vintage fabrics in the bedroom. Once you have bought your fabrics and bed linen, wash it well. If you feel the need to use a detergent, test the fabric first to see if it is colorfast, as many vintage fabrics were created using natural dyes that might still run. Try a patch test, with a little of the detergent rubbed on a corner that will not show, and leave it to dry to see if there is any dramatic fading or dye-seepage. You can also use wool soap for a more gentle wash that will not fade your fabric as much. However, most well-worn fabrics can be washed thoroughly, having been laundered countless times through the generations. For family bedrooms, choose a cotton that can be washed at high temperatures, especially when using old mattress ticking. Comforters or eiderdowns can be cleaned in the washing machine, but for a plumper finish, finish off in a tumble dryer. If you are nervous about using your antique bedlinens, then seek out a modern-day replica; mingled with an antique bedspread or quilted cushions, it will be hard to tell which of your linen layers is the older.

Above: reproduction scarlet checks taken from an antique French design. All the fabrics here are re-used scraps from hard-wearing natural materials—a piece of old linen sewn to a lampshade, a child's hair-ribbon, patches of cotton for wardrobe doors, a hand-knit sweater and a stool cover from deckchair ticking; proof indeed that a bargain can be stylish.

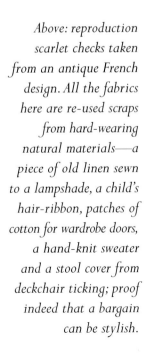

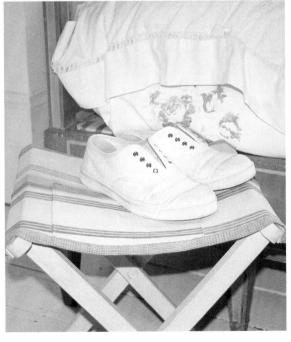

Index

Cabbages and Roses

St. Catherine

Bath

United Kingdom

BA1 8HA

Telephone: +44 (0) 1225 859151

Fax: +44 (0) 1225 852072

www.cabbagesandroses.com

acknowledgments

A million thank yous to all the people who aided and abetted in the production of this book. Special thanks to Kate, for not minding me working on a beach on the south coast when I should have been collecting her from the airport on her return from the Far East, to Edward who has cooked us feasts and made us laugh after a long day's work and to Mark, my rock, for always being there.   And to....

Kate Barton, Mel Bourne, Brigette Buchanan, Maudie Buchanan, Sarah Cooper, Anthea Craigmyle, Maureen Docherty, Clare Faull, Katy Forman, Lucy Fry, Tony and Sabrina Fry, Georgina Harris, Sarah Hoggett, Max Linham, Pia Maclean, Prudence Macleod, Penny Menato, Cindy Richards, Karin and Nick Southorn, Matthew Tugwell, Edina van der Wyck (for beautiful photographs and making me laugh), Cassie Wilkinson, and Alice and Laura Woodroff.